our United Nations

Foreword

Welcome to the United Nations. This is your Organization. These buildings and grounds that form the Headquarters of the United Nations belong to you, the peoples of the world.

When the United Nations came into existence in 1945, after the end of the Second World War, "We the peoples"—the opening words of the Charter—meant the representatives of the fifty nations who had gathered at San Francisco, determined "to save succeeding generations from the scourge of war".

Today, more than three times that number of States are members of the United Nations, representing almost all the peoples of the world. They have joined the Organization with a pledge to work together in the search for peace, justice and progress and to use the United Nations as a "centre for harmonizing the actions of nations" in the attainment of these common ends.

The delegates—representatives of Member States—who meet in the General Assembly Hall, the Council chambers and the conference rooms that you will be visiting, and the men and women from many countries who serve in the Secretariat, are working to achieve the goals of the Charter and to bring about a better life for all mankind. Your understanding and support of their efforts is vital to the success of the United Nations.

[signature]

Javier Pérez de Cuéllar, Secretary-General

Introduction

The United Nations, an organization of sovereign nations representing almost all of humanity, has as its central goal the maintenance of international peace and security.

Its other main purposes under the Charter are to develop friendly relations among nations based on respect for the equal rights and self-determination of peoples; to co-operate in solving international economic, social, cultural and humanitarian problems and in promoting human rights for all; and to be a centre for harmonizing the actions of nations in attaining these ends.

There are many examples where the United Nations has played, and continues to play, an active role in reducing tensions, preventing conflicts or putting an end to fighting already under way. And quite apart from security or politically related problems, there is today a whole range of challenges which can only be dealt with through international co-operation—energy, the environment, outer space, the sea-bed, economic and social development, international trade and many other areas of world concern.

There are six main organs of the United Nations—the *General Assembly,* the *Security Council,* the *Economic and Social Council,* the *Trusteeship Council,* the *International Court of Justice* and the *Secretariat.* All are based at United Nations Headquarters in New York, except the Court, which is located at The Hague, in the Netherlands. While Headquarters is the diplomatic crossroads of the world, the United Nations "family" of organizations, programmes and staff are at work all over the globe.

Soon after the signing of the United Nations Charter in San Francisco, in 1945, a key decision of the first General Assembly session was to place the permanent headquarters of the Organization in the United States. Subsequently, many sites were considered, but when, in December 1946, the American philanthropist and financier John D. Rockefeller, Jr., offered a gift of $8.5 million to purchase the East River site in New York City, the General Assembly quickly accepted. New York City acquired and gave to the United Nations adjacent land needed to round out the site and ceded streets and waterfront rights along the East River. The city also contributed generously to a programme of improvements in the area.

On entering the iron gates at United Nations Plaza, one experiences the feeling of something distinctly different. The colourful echelon of flags of Member States proclaims that this 16-acre tract of trees, gardens and buildings, peopled by men and women from every corner of the globe, belongs not to one nation but to all.

The four buildings which comprise the United Nations Headquarters are: the low, domed *General Assembly Building*; the 39-storey glass and marble *Secretariat Building*; the low, rectangular *Conference Building* along the East River; and the *Dag Hammarskjöld Library* at the southwest corner of the site.

Occupancy of the Secretariat Building began in 1950, but it was not until 1952 that the first meetings could be held in the General Assembly Hall, the Council chambers and the conference rooms. Construction costs, exclusive of the Library, were approximately $67 million, of which $65 million was financed by an interest-free loan from the United States. The Dag Hammarskjöld Library, built at a cost of $6.6 million, was a gift of the Ford Foundation.

The basic design of the Headquarters was the work of an international team of architects headed by Wallace K. Harrison of the United States. This Board of Design, as it was called, worked with two fundamental principles in mind: to plan the most efficient working space for both staff and delegates and, at the same time, to create—within the limitations set by functional requirements and available funds—an aesthetic and architecturally co-ordinated group of buildings.

Works of art abound at the United Nations, both inside and outside the buildings, reflecting the desire of Member States and individuals to beautify the Headquarters with representative contributions. In the gardens, mainly to the north of the buildings and along the river, the many trees and other plantings are also the gifts of individuals and groups from many lands.

The visitors' entrance to the United Nations is through the gates at the northern end of the Headquarters site, into the lobby of the General Assembly Building, with its clean, modern lines of cantilevered balconies and soft lights.
01

Flags of all Member States, arranged in alphabetical order, fly in a row along United Nations Plaza, providing a colourful welcome to Headquarters. In the foreground is a circular fountain, flanked by a large bronze sculpture by the English artist Barbara Hepworth entitled "Single Form", erected in memory of Dag Hammarskjöld.
02

About half a million people each year visit United Nations Headquarters, which has long been a major tourist attraction. Here, one of the guides leads a group of visitors on a tour through the buildings, pointing out its many features and giving a brief outline of the Organization's history and activities. Guides from some 30 countries conduct these popular tours, which are open to the public seven days a week.
03

United Nations Headquarters, in New York, occupies a 16-acre tract of land on Manhattan's East Side, extending from 42nd to 48th Streets between the East River and United Nations Plaza (a stretch of First Avenue). The Headquarters complex is dominated by the 39-storey Secretariat Building, which is flanked by the low, domed General Assembly Building and, in the foreground, the Dag Hammarskjöld Library. The Headquarters site, which is international territory, is the nerve centre for the world-wide activities of the United Nations.
04

The General Assembly

The General Assembly, sometimes called the nearest thing to a "parliament of mankind", is the main deliberative organ of the United Nations. It has the right to discuss and make recommendations on all matters within the scope of the Charter. It deals with virtually every topic of broad human concern—issues of war and peace, world economic problems calling for international co-operation, the struggle of peoples under colonial rule and the aspirations of all people to exercise their basic rights, threats to human existence from armaments and pollution, and the vast potential benefits of scientific and technological progress.

All Members of the United Nations are represented in the General Assembly, and each nation has one vote. The Assembly has no power to compel action by any nation, but its recommendations carry a moral weight which no Government can easily ignore.

Its regular sessions are held for mid-September to mid-December each year, but it can be convened in special or emergency sessions for matters of immediate concern. When the Security Council fails to act on a threat to peace because of a veto, the Assembly may be called into session to deal with the problem, at the request of the Council or by a majority vote of the members of the United Nations.

The Assembly establishes goals in the field of development, organizes conferences on major issues and makes recommendations on problems ranging from the danger of nuclear arms to the injustice of racism. Holding a central position in the Organization, it receives reports from all other organs, admits new Members (on the recommendation of the Security Council), approves the budget, appoints the Secretary-General and members of other organs, and guides the work programmes of the Secretariat.

Decisions and resolutions of the General Assembly on questions of world-wide concern have led progressively to the adoption of internationally binding conventions and treaties, such as the international conventions on political, economic and social rights, the treaties on the non-proliferation of nuclear weapons and on nuclear-free zones and, most recently, the Convention on the Law of the Sea.

View of the General Assembly Hall. There are more than 2,000 seats—1,092 for delegations of Member States, 663 for alternates and other representatives, 53 for the news media and 280 for the public. The Hall itself is enormous, 165 feet by 115 feet, with a 75-foot-high ceiling.
05

Delegates gather outside the Assembly Hall before the start of a plenary meeting.
06

As new States are admitted to membership in the United Nations, they take their place in the General Assembly. Here, the representatives of the new nation of Saint Vincent and the Grenadines are seated for the first time in the Assembly Hall.
07

The General Assembly

Secretary-General Javier Pérez de Cuéllar addressing the General Assembly on 10 October 1986 after his appointment by acclamation to a second five-year term as Secretary-General of the United Nations.
08

A voting console linked to each delegate's desk on the floor of the Assembly Hall and to panels listing the name of each Member State records and simultaneously counts votes as they are cast. Voting may also be by secret ballot.
09

Six languages are used officially in the General Assembly—Arabic, Chinese, English, French, Russian and Spanish. All seats in the Assembly—and in the Council chambers and conference rooms—are equipped with earphones which can be tuned to the speaker on the floor or at the podium or to a simultaneous interpretation in the official languages. Here the interpreters can be seen at work in their glass-enclosed booths overlooking the Security Council.
10

The agenda for the General Assembly's regular session usually contains more than 100 items, which are debated in plenary meetings or in the seven main committees of the Assembly. Hundreds of documents—reports, drafts, studies—on the questions under discussion are distributed and read each day by the delegates before resolutions on them come to a vote in plenary. The decisions of the Assembly govern the expenditures and activities of the Organization.
11

In the Delegates' Lounge, adjacent to the General Assembly Hall, delegates meet informally and confer, and often reach agreement on issues before votes are taken in the Assembly. On the wall, right, is a gigantic tapestry depicting the Great Wall of China.
12

The Security Council

The United Nations organ which has primary responsibility for maintaining international peace and security is the Security Council.

The Council has 15 members. Five of these—China, France, the Soviet Union, the United Kingdom and the United States—are permanent members. The other ten are elected by the General Assembly every two years.

Each member of the Council has one vote. Decisions on matters of procedure are made by an affirmative vote of at least nine of the 15 members. Decisions on substantive matters also require nine votes, including the concurring votes of all five permanent members. This is the rule of "great Power unanimity", often referred to as the "veto". All five permanent members have exercised the veto right at one time or another. If a permanent member does not support a decision but has no desire to block it through a veto, it may abstain.

Under the Charter, all Members of the United Nations agree to accept and carry out the decisions of the Council. While other organs of the United Nations make recommendations to Governments, the Council alone has the power to take decisions which Member States are obligated under the Charter to carry out. The Council has the right to investigate any dispute or situation which might lead to friction between two or more countries. When a complaint concerning a threat to peace is brought before it, the Council's first action is usually to recommend that the parties try to reach agreement by peaceful means. In some cases, the Council itself undertakes investigation or mediation. It may appoint special representatives, or request the Secretary-General to use his good offices. In certain cases it may set forth principles for a peaceful settlement.

When a dispute leads to fighting, the Council's first concern is to bring this to an end as soon as possible. Over the decades since its establishment, the Council has issued many cease-fire directives which have been instrumental in preventing wide hostilities in various parts of the world. The Council may decide on enforcement measures, economic sanctions (such as trade embargoes) or collective military action. Sometimes it sends peace-keeping forces to help reduce tensions in troubled areas and keep opposing forces apart.

A general view of the Security Council in session. The Council chamber was designed by the Norwegian architect Arnstein Arneberg, and most of the furnishings are gifts from the Norwegian Government. The large mural, by Per Krohg of Norway, symbolizes the promise of future peace and individual freedom.

13

The Security Council has 15 members, five permanent and ten elected every two years. The Presidency of the Council changes on the first of each month, rotating in the English alphabetical order of the names of each member country. Formal votes are taken by a show of hands.
14

In the Security Council, consultations often lead to agreement before a formal vote is called.
15

The United Nations Peace-keeping Force in Cyprus, established by the Security Council in 1964, now numbers some 2,300 men from eight countries. It supervises the cease-fire between the Cyprus National Guard and the Turkish armed forces, supports humanitarian activities and looks after the welfare and safety of Greek Cypriots in the northern part of the island, while talks between the Greek and Turkish Cypriot communities continue.
16

United Nations peace-keeping forces have been stationed in the Middle East for more than two decades as the search continues for a peaceful solution to the political problems underlying the conflict there. The United Nations Interim Force in Lebanon, shown here, was established by the Security Council in 1978 to bring about the withdrawal of Israeli forces from southern Lebanon and to help the Lebanese Government re-establish its authority in the area.

17

The United Nations Emergency Force, shown here crossing the Suez Canal in 1973, was established by the Security Council in that year to assist in the disengagement of forces in the Egypt-Israel sector. Following the signing of a peace treaty between Egypt and Israel in 1979, the Force was withdrawn, but two other peace-keeping groups remained in the area: the United Nations Disengagement Observer Force, in the Israel-Syria sector, and the United Nations Truce Supervision Organization.

18

The Economic and Social Council

Most of the work of the United Nations, measured in terms of money and personnel, goes into the varied programmes aimed at achieving, in the words of the Charter, "better standards of life in larger freedom" for all peoples.

Working under the authority of the General Assembly, the Economic and Social Council co-ordinates the economic and social development work of the United Nations and its related agencies and institutions—known as the "United Nations family" of organizations. It also has responsibility for the promotion of human rights for all peoples.
The range of economic and social development activities undertaken by the United Nations has steadily increased, in response to the recognized needs of the developing countries, many of them former colonial territories that have attained independence and joined the United Nations as sovereign States. For many of these countries, the most pressing problems today are how to develop their economic resources, educate their people, improve housing and health services, modernize transport and communications and obtain the benefits of modern science and technology. Helping Governments find answers to these and other questions is among the Council's tasks.

In the face of the widening gulf between the industrially advanced societies and the developing countries, the General Assembly, in 1974, adopted a Declaration and a Programme of Action on the Establishment of a New International Economic Order, focusing on the need for radical changes in existing international economic relations in order to narrow the gap between developed and developing countries.

In December 1980, the Assembly adopted an International Development Strategy for the Third United Nations Development Decade (1981-1990), which sets targets for developing countries that include an average annual increase of 7 per cent in gross domestic product and of 7.5-8 per cent in international trade, and which calls on each developed country to contribute at least 1 per cent of its gross national product to help developing countries.

The Economic and Social Council, seen here in session, has 54 members and generally meets twice a year for periods of about one month. The Council chamber was designed by Sven Markelius of Sweden and was furnished by that country.
19

On the front line of the effort to promote economic and social progress is the United Nations Development Programme, which, in co-operation with the United Nations family of agencies and institutions, works with governments of developing countries in carrying out high-priority development projects. UNDP is the world's largest single source of multinational technical co-operation aid, helping poorer countries to attract capital needed for large-scale development activities and to use all available resources as effectively as possible.

Many of these development and related projects are carried out by the United Nations itself, with the aid of the five regional commissions—for Africa; Asia and the Pacific; Western Asia; Europe; and Latin America and the Caribbean—and through the work of other specialized institutions of the United Nations concerned with such questions as the welfare of children and of refugees, world food problems, industrial development and international trade, the environment, housing and community development, disaster relief, crime prevention, the status of women, and population questions.

Some of these questions have long been of concern to various United Nations organs, such as UNICEF and the World Food Programme. Others have been given greater emphasis through the more recent establishment of special programmes and funds, such as the United Nations Fund for Population Activities, the United Nations Environment Programme and HABITAT, both located in Nairobi, Kenya, and the Office of the United Nations Disaster Relief Co-ordinator.

The achievement of universal literacy and improved educational standards for all peoples are among the goals of the United Nations Educational, Scientific and Cultural Organization. Seen here, Mexican boys outside their classroom in Chiapas.
20

Health for all by the year 2000 is the goal of the World Health Organization, which has already seen the complete eradication of smallpox throughout the world. Here, a health inspector takes a blood sample from a Somalian child, as part of a campaign aimed at eradicating malaria.
21

The victims of war and political unrest are often the innocent—mothers and children, the elderly, the sick and disabled—uprooted from their homes or forced to seek asylum in other countries. Care and resettlement of refugees has been a continuing concern of the United Nations, through the programmes of the United Nations High Commissioner for Refugees, the United Nations Relief and Works Agency for Palestine Refugees in the Near East and other agencies. Seen here, are Lebanese refugees in a camp in Beirut.
22

Food production—including development of new sources of protein and improved methods of crop-growing and harvesting—is the major concern of the Food and Agriculture Organization of the United Nations. A fish catch is readied for market at Cochin, in India's Kerala State; Bananas are harvested on a plantation in Coto Sur, Costa Rica.

23

24

For some time to come, the poorer countries of the world will have to rely on agriculture to raise their living standards and supply the capital they need to create industries. Agricultural production must therefore be increased. This requires tractors, fertilizers, new and better seeds, vast irrigation schemes and land reform, to replace age-old farming ways. Seen here, a farmer transplanting rice and women working on a farm near Dhaka, Bangladesh.

24

25

25

Programmes aimed at the attainment of decent housing, in both urban and rural areas, and adequate sanitation and water supply facilities have become an increasingly large part of United Nations technical co-operation activities in developing countries.

Children load and carry bricks in Colombia, and fill a water bucket in Thailand. Mud-cement bricks are used for housebuilding in Burkina Faso.
25

Industrial development and population growth increase the demand for more power and water. The hydroelectric dam in Ghana, shown here, was built with assistance from the United Nations Development Programme.
26

A meteorologist in Costa Rica replaces a recording chart on a sun gauge, part of a weather and water watch programme administered by the World Meteorological Organization to provide vital information on the region's water distribution and supply.
27

Development of transport and communications is one of the developing countries' primary needs.
28

27

28

The improvement of ports and harbours, and of shipping and transport facilities, is vital for the trade of developing countries. Here, freighters unload their cargoes at the port of Tunis, in Tunisia, and at dockyards in Calcutta, India.
29

The Trusteeship Council

Under the Charter, the Trusteeship Council was assigned the task of supervising the administration of territories which were placed under the International Trusteeship System, the major goals of which were to promote the advancement of the inhabitants of the Trust Territories and their progressive development towards self-government or independence.

The aims of the Trusteeship System have been fulfilled to such an extent that by 1975 only one of the original 11 Trust Territories remained—the Pacific Islands (administered by the United States). The others, mostly in Africa, had attained independence—either as separate States or by joining neighbouring independent countries—following a period of Trusteeship Council supervision. The 10 former Trust Territories were: Australian-administered Nauru (now the Republic of Nauru) and New Guinea (now Papua New Guinea); Belgian-administered Ruanda-Urundi (now Rwanda and Burundi); French Cameroons (now Cameroon) and French Togoland (now Togo); Italian Somaliland (now part of Somalia); New Zealand-administered Western Samoa (now Samoa); and British Cameroons (now part of Nigeria and Cameroon), Tanganyika (with Zanzibar, now the United Republic of Tanzania) and British Togoland (now part of Ghana).

Despite the gains made under the Trusteeship System, however, there remained many other areas in the world still under colonial rule—in Africa, the Caribbean, South-East Asia and the islands of the Pacific, Atlantic and Indian Oceans. Under the Charter, States responsible for administering these territories accepted the principle that the interests of the inhabitants were paramount, and they undertook to ensure the political, economic, social and educational advancement of the peoples under their administration and their progressive development towards self-government or independence.

In the Trusteeship Council Chamber a light and harmonious effect is achieved through the use of fine woods and contrasting colours. The Chamber was designed by Finn Juhl of Denmark, and the furnishings were provided by the Danish Government. The statue on the far wall was carved from teak by Henrik Starcke, also of Denmark.

30

The move towards independence was greatly accelerated in 1960 by the landmark decision of the General Assembly to adopt the Declaration on the Granting of Independence to Colonial Countries and Peoples, which proclaimed the necessity of bringing colonialism in all its forms and manifestations to a speedy and unconditional end. The following year, the Assembly established the Special Committee on decolonization to follow implementation of the Declaration. Since its adoption, more than 50 former territories have become independent, and fewer than 20 territories still remain under colonial rule.

Today, the last stronghold of minority and foreign domination in the world is in southern Africa. In South Africa, the *apartheid* (racial segregation) system, which denies political and other rights to the vast majority of the country's inhabitants, has been denounced by the General Assembly as "a crime against humanity". In Namibia (formerly South West Africa), the vast territory for which the United Nations assumed responsibility in 1966 when it revoked South Africa's League of Nations mandate over the territory and established the United Nations Council for Namibia as the legal administering authority for the territory until independence, the United Nations has called for South Africa's withdrawal and for the achievement of Namibian independence through free elections under United Nations supervision and control.

Centuries-old colonial rule in Africa was nearly ended by 1980 with the achievement of independence of the former Portuguese territories of Angola, Cape Verde, Guinea-Bissau, Mozambique, and Sao Tome and Principe and of the former British colony of Southern Rhodesia, which became independent as Zimbabwe. Seen here are schoolchildren on Sao Tiago Island, Cape Verde, during a visit by a United Nations mission shortly before the country's independence in 1975.
31

In southern Africa, Namibia still remained a colonial territory, despite adoption by the Security Council in 1978 of a plan for self-determination and independence for the Namibian people. Below, Herero women at Okahandja, one of Namibia's main cities north of Windhoek, attend a funeral ceremony for a chief assassinated by terrorists.
32

Students from the Islamic Cultural Centre parade through the football stadium in Mogadiscio, Somalia, on independence day—1 July 1960. Since 1960, when the General Assembly adopted a historic declaration on decolonization, more than 50 former colonies have joined the United Nations as independent sovereign States.
33

A group of women in the southern part of the former Portuguese territory of Guinea-Bissau listen to a statement by a special United Nations mission which visited the liberated areas in April 1972. The independence of Guinea-Bissau was proclaimed on 24 September 1973.
34

The Dag Hammarskjöld Library

The Dag Hammarskjöld Library at United Nations Head-quarters, financed by a gift of $6.6 million from the Ford Foundation, consists of six storeys, three above ground and three below—and a penthouse. The Library was dedicated in November 1961 in honour of Dag Hammarskjöld, Secretary-General of the United Nations from 1953 until his death in September 1961.

The Library serves as a reference centre for use by delegates, staff members and accredited members of the press and of organizations. Its holdings are limited to materials, in many languages, bearing on the interests of the United Nations—political, legal, social, economic and geographical conditions in all nations of the world. They total close to 400,000 volumes, an increasing number of which are available on microfilm.

Most of the Library collections are devoted to the documents and publications of the United Nations and the specialized agencies. The Woodrow Wilson Reading Room houses an important collection of books dealing with the League of Nations, together with books about international relations during the period between the two world wars. The Map Room contains about 70,000 maps and a library of atlases, gazetteers, guides and other reference works in many languages.

In addition to reading rooms, the Library has a 200-seat auditorium equipped with a screen and footlights and with equipment for sound and simultaneous interpretation. The Periodical Room is stocked with current issues of several thousand periodicals and hundreds of newspapers from all over the world.

Because of its specialized nature, the Library is not open to the general public, but researchers may apply for permission to use its services.

The Dag Hammarskjöld Library

The Works of Art and the Gardens

Because these buildings belong to all Member nations, many countries have naturally wished to beautify them with works of art, presented by governments on behalf of their countries or by private groups and individuals. These gifts range from small pictures to vast murals, from delicate carvings to large statues and from art of 3,000 years ago to that of today. They are displayed in the corridors and conference rooms, in the entrance lobbies and in the gardens.

The United Nations Gardens, located mainly to the north of the Headquarters buildings, along the East River, contain many trees and other plantings donated by groups and individuals—honey locusts, sweet gums, pin oaks, hawthorns, and espaliered fruit trees. The gardens are particularly beautiful in spring when the daffodils are out and the cherry trees are in bloom. The rose garden with its many varieties of tea roses selected from show winners is in bloom from early summer into fall.

Stained glass window by French artist Marc Chagall, located outside the Meditation Room in the General Assembly public lobby, depicts the artist's conceptions on the theme of "Peace and Man".

38

39

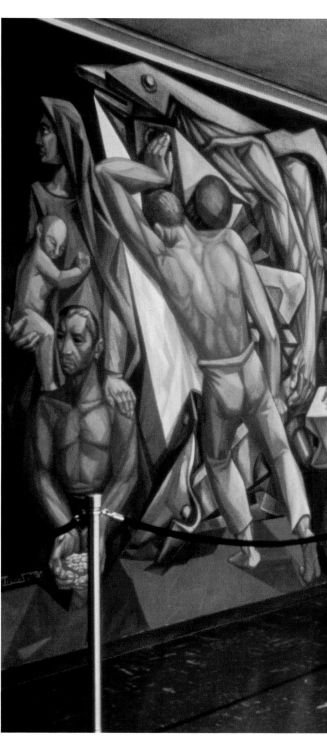

40

A third-century Tunisian mosaic depicting the cycle of the year is mounted at entrance to the Delegates' Lounge.
39

An ancient amphora from Cyprus, dating from 600-700 B.C., is displayed in the corridor of the Conference Building.
40

A mural by Spanish artist José Vela Zanetti, depicting man's struggle for peace, is located in the Conference Building.
41

42

44

Portraits of former Secretaries-General of the United Nations: Trygve Lie, of Norway, the first Secretary-General (1946-1953); Dag Hammarskjöld, of Sweden, Secretary-General from 1953 to 1961; U Thant, of Burma, Secretary-General from 1961 to 1971; and Kurt Waldheim, of Austria, Secretary-General from 1972 to 1981.

Trygve Lie, by Norwegian artist Harald Dal.
42

Dag Hammarskjöld, by Swedish artist Bo Beskow.
43

U Thant, by American artist James Whitney.
44

Kurt Waldheim, by American artist Everett Raymond Kinstler.
45

Replica of a 13th-century Bulgarian fresco. The original was painted inside Boyana church near Sofia.
46

Mural tapestry, "Triumph of Peace", designed by Belgian artist Peter Colfe and one of the largest ever woven, hangs above stairway of the Delegates' Lobby. To left of stairway is "Peace", one of two murals depicting war and peace by Brazilian artist Candido Portinari.
47

The bronze equestrian statue symbolizing Peace is by the Yugoslav sculptor Anton Augustincic. The ornamental iron fence, through which the statue is seen, surrounds the grounds of the United Nations buildings and is a gift of the City of New York.
48

In the North Garden, a bronze statue by the Soviet sculptor Evgeny Vuchetich entitled "We Shall Beat Our Swords into Plowshares".
49

48

49

Japanese Peace Bell, cast from coins and metal donated by people of 60 nations and housed in a Shinto-like shrine, is set in landscaped area north-west of the Secretariat Building.
50

Wooden Balinese statue symbolizing "Peace".
51

Oil painting, "Christ Crucified", by French artist Georges Rouault, was a gift from Pope Paul VI.
52

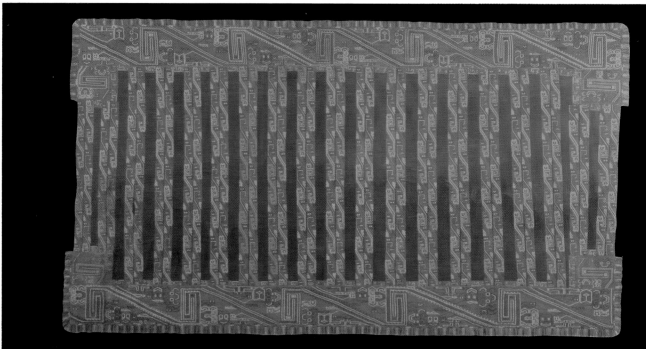

Mural tapestry, "Ode to Man", by Romanian artist Ion Nicodin, hangs in the Delegates' Lounge.
53

Peruvian ceremonial mantle, used by the Incas in the burial of their kings.
54

View of the rose garden.
55

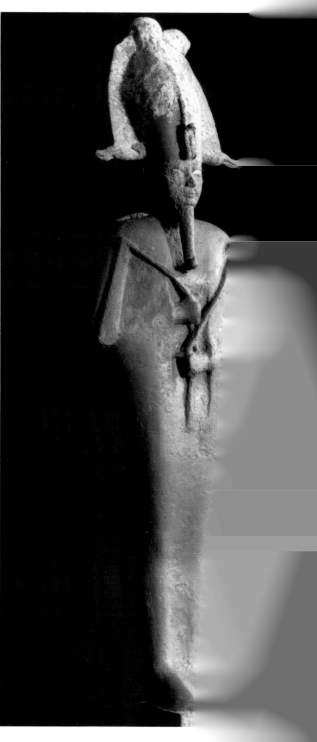

In the North Garden, a bronze statue by sculptor Fritz Cremer of the German Democractic Republic entitled "The Rising Man".
56

A 2,700-year-old statuette of the Egyptian god Osiris.
57

A mural tapestry, "Maaggala Tuubaa" ("Pilgrimage to Tuba"), by Senegalese artist Papa Ibra Tall hangs in foyer of the General Assembly Building.
58

A mosaic depicting "The Dove of Peace" was a gift from Pope John Paul II on the occasion of his visit to the United Nations in 1979.
59

58

59

"Femme sur l'échelle" ("Woman on a Ladder"), tapestry woven from a painting by Pablo Picasso.
60

The Japanese cherry trees and the daffodils, and most of the other trees and plantings in the United Nations Gardens, were donated by groups and individuals.
61

The Secretariat

More than 15,500 men and women from some 150 countries are employed by the United Nations Secretariat—about one third of them at Headquarters and the other two thirds in United Nations offices and centres around the globe—and another 10,500 work for the various United Nations organs. Many have had distinguished careers in their own countries, but when they join the United Nations they cease to serve their own governments and instead serve the world Organization.

Among the staff, working for the most part "behind the scenes" at Headquarters, are linguists, economists, editors, social scientists, legal experts, librarians, journalists, statisticians, broadcasters, personnel officers, administrators and experts in all the varied fields of activity covered by the United Nations. They prepare reports and studies requested by various United Nations bodies; issue press releases and produce publications, broadcasts and films giving information about the Organization; and perform the administrative duties needed to implement resolutions adopted by the various organs. In addition, there are clerks, stenographers, typists, word processors, messengers, maintenance engineers and technicians, as well as a corps of officers in blue-grey uniforms who are responsible for the security of the Headquarters complex.

The head of this multinational staff is the Secretary-General of the United Nations, who is appointed by the General Assembly every five years. The first Secretary-General was Trygve Lie, of Norway. He was succeeded by Dag Hammarskjöld, of Sweden, in 1953. After the death of Dag Hammarskjöld in a plane crash in Africa on 18 September 1961, U Thant, of Burma, was appointed Acting Secretary-General to fill out the rest of Mr. Hammarskjöld's term. U Thant was formally appointed Secretary-General in 1962 and served two five-year terms (1961-1971). He was succeeded by Kurt Waldheim, of Austria, who also served two terms (1972-1981). The present Secretary-General, appointed on 15 December 1981, is Javier Pérez de Cuéllar, of Peru.

On the lower levels of the General Assembly Building are studios for radio and television broadcasts, a film and record library and a master sound control room. Here, a live television transmission of a Security Council meeting is sent overseas via satellite.

62

The Secretary-General carries direct and personal responsibility for the work of the whole Secretariat. He submits an annual report on the work of the Organization to the General Assembly. Under the Charter, the Secretary-General has the right to bring to the attention of the Security Council any matter which in his opinion may threaten the maintenance of international peace and security. As the demands on the United Nations peace-making and peace-keeping machinery have increased through the years, so has the Secretary-General's role in the diplomatic sphere and in the exercise of his "good offices" to help resolve problems not only in the political but also in humanitarian and other spheres.

The United Nations produces an enormous volume of printed materials, ranging from one-page information leaflets to multi-volume conference proceedings. The Reproduction Section of the Publishing Division often works around the clock.
63

The language laboratories give staff members the opportunity to improve their proficiency in any of the six working languages of the United Nations — Arabic, Chinese, English, French, Russian and Spanish.
64

Electronic data processing and information systems help meet the Organization's increasing needs for processing and storing statistical and other data and for many other scientific and administrative tasks.
65

How the UN Story Is Told

Ever since the establishment of the United Nations, it has been recognized that an informed world public opinion is one of the greatest sources of strength that the Organization could draw upon. Accordingly, and in keeping with the wishes of the membership, every effort is made to assure a steady flow of information to the peoples of the world. At Headquarters, special facilities and services are provided for the hundreds of press, radio and television correspondents who regularly cover the United Nations "beat". Overseas, there are more than 60 United Nations Information Centres in as many countries disseminating information— as far as possible in the languages of the countries served—to newspapers, radio stations, non-governmental organizations, schools and other interested groups.

Secretary-General Javier Pérez de Cuéllar holding a press conference at Kalahari Sands Hotel in Windhoek on 26 August 1983.

66

67

69

United Nations Secretary-General Javier Pérez de Cuéllar meets frequently with the press. Here he videotapes three special statements for the International Year of Peace.
67

News service photographers cover a General Assembly meeting.
68

Non-governmental organizations play a vital role in supporting the United Nations, disseminating information about the Organization and participating actively in its work. Here, at a ceremony held at United Nations Headquarters on 10 June 1982, at the start of the General Assembly's second special session on disarmament, the Secretary-General addresses a crowd of over 1,000 as he was formally presented with disarmament petitions from 20 non-governmental organizations, signed by over 100 million people.
69

Stamps issued by the United Nations Postal Administration illustrate the aims as well as the various aspects of the work of the world Organization. The stamps are printed by security printers throughout the world and are designed by artists representing more than 60 countries. Issued in United States, Swiss and Austrian denominations, the stamps can be used for mailing only from United Nations Headquarters in New York, the Palais des Nations in Geneva or the Vienna International Centre, respectively.
70

Offices and Services Away from Headquarters

While United Nations Headquarters in New York serves as the nerve-centre of the Organization's far-flung operations, a growing number of important activities are concentrated in offices overseas. These include:

—In Europe: the International Court of Justice, one of the main organs of the United Nations, which has its seat at The Hague, in the Netherlands; the European Office of the United Nations, in Geneva, Switzerland, which is also the home of the Economic Commission for Europe and of a number of specialized agencies; and the Vienna International Centre, in Vienna, Austria, headquarters of the United Nations Industrial Development Organization, the United Nations Relief and Works Agency for Palestine Refugees in the Near East and a number of other United Nations organs and agencies;

—In Africa: the Economic Commission for Africa, in Addis Ababa, Ethiopia; and the United Nations Environment Programme and the United Nations Centre for Human Settlements, both in Nairobi, Kenya;

—In Asia: the Economic and Social Commission for Asia and the Pacific, in Bangkok, Thailand; and the Economic and Social Commission for Western Asia, in Baghdad, Iraq;

—In Latin America: the Economic Commission for Latin America and the Caribbean and the Latin American Institute for Economic and Social Planning, in Santiago, Chile.

Aerial view of the Palais des Nations, overlooking "Lac Leman" in Geneva, Switzerland. The European Office of the United Nations is the home of several United Nations organs and specialized agencies.
71

The Vienna International Centre, built by the Austrian Government at a cost of $700 million and offered rent-free to the United Nations and its agencies, can accommodate 1,600 people in its conference halls and about 5,000 office workers.
73

The United Nations building complex in Santiago, Chile, houses the Economic Commission for Latin America and the Caribbean and the Latin American Institute for Economic and Social Planning.
72

74

75

Nairobi, Kenya, is the headquarters of the United Nations Environment Programme, seen here, and the United Nations Centre for Human Settlements (HABITAT).
74

The headquarters of the Economic and Social Commission for Asia and the Pacific, in Bangkok, Thailand, comprises a 14-storey secretariat building, a seven-storey service building and a conference area.
75

The Economic Commission for Africa has its headquarters in these buildings at Addis Ababa, Ethiopia, completed and occupied in 1961.
76

77

77

Design of the new headquarters of the Economic and Social Commission for Western Asia, in Baghad, Iraq.
77

The International Court of Justice, the principal judicial organ of the United Nations, holds virtually all its sessions at its headquarters at The Hague, in the Netherlands.
78

Photo Credits: F. Botts, Ted Chen, David Dewhurst, Peter Fraenkel, Bill Graham, Rick Grunbaum, Milton Grant, Jean Pierre Lafont, John Isaac, David Mangurian, Saw Lwin, George Prayne, Yutaka Nagata, Michael Tzovaras, Edward Rice, M. S. Essakalli, Bachrach, Ray Witlin, Carl Purcell

A Few Facts and Figures
Answers to some of the questions frequently asked by visitors

The Headquarters site is owned by the United Nations and is international territory. Under special agreement with the United States, certain privileges and immunities have been granted, but generally the laws of New York City, New York State and the United States apply.

Most signs throughout the Headquarters are in English and French, two of the "working languages" of the Organization.

The regular budget of the United Nations is paid by assessed contributions from Member States, but most of its assistance programmes are funded through voluntary contributions.

In terms of population, the largest United Nations Member is China (over 1 billion) and the smallest, Saint Christopher and Nevis (45,000).

United Nations Day is celebrated each year on 24 October because on that day in 1945 the Charter came into force.

The oldest members of the United Nations family of organizations are the International Telecommunication Union (established in 1865) and the Universal Postal Union (1875).

The largest military force organized under the direct command of the United Nations was the Congo Force, which had a peak strength of nearly 20,000 men.

United Nations technical assistance to developing countries began in 1948 with an appropriation of $350,000. Today, the United Nations Development Programme alone helps finance development activities valued at over $1.4 billion a year.

Approximately 50,000 requests from the public for information on the United Nations are answered each year.

More than 30 million visitors have taken guided tours of the Headquarters, offered in more than 23 languages.

United Nations Sales Number 87.I.
ISBN 92-1-100315-6
Copyright © United Nations 1987
All rights reserved
Manufactured in U.S.A.